Cities through Time

Daily Life in Ancient and Modern

ISTANBUL

by Robert Bator

illustrations by Chris Rothero

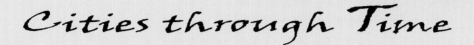

Runestone Press/Minneapolis
A Division of Lerner Publishing Group

The *Cities through Time* series is produced by Runestone Press, a division of Lerner Publishing Group, in cooperation with Greenleaf Publishing, Inc., Geneva, Illinois.

Text design by Melanie Lawson, Jean DeVaty, and Rebecca JonMichaels. Cover design by Michael Tacheny.

Runestone Press
A Division of Lerner Publishing Group
241 First Avenue North
Minneapolis, Minnesota 55401 U.S.A.

Website address: www.lernerbooks.com

Library of Congress Cataloging-in-Publication Data

Bator, Robert.
    Daily life in ancient and modern Istanbul / by Robert Bator;
illustrated by Chris Rothero
      p. cm. — (Cities through time)
    Includes index.
    Summary: A historical exploration of events and daily life in
Istanbul in both ancient and modern times.
    ISBN 0–8225–3217–4 (lib. bdg.)
    1. Istanbul (Turkey)—Social life and customs—Juvenile
literature. [1. Istanbul (Turkey)] I. Rothero, Chris, ill. II. Title.
III. Series.
    DR726.B38 2000
    949.61'8—dc21   98–53959

Manufactured in the United States of America
1 2 3 4 5 6 – JR – 05 04 03 02 01 00

Contents

The heavens may turn about the world as they will. They will find no city like Istanbul.
—Nabi, seventeenth-century Turkish poet

Introduction

Istanbul was once the capital of Turkey. It remains the most important city in Turkey—a large, peninsular nation that forms a bridge between southeastern Europe and Asia. Istanbul is basically a European city with Asian suburbs. Located on the small European portion of Turkey, the city is separated from Asian Turkey by the narrow Bosporus Strait. The Turks call Asian Turkey "Anatolia."

From the very beginning, geography shaped Istanbul's destiny. Located on a high point of land surrounded by water on three sides, the city controlled a vital sea route that carried ships from the Black Sea to the Aegean Sea. It also lay where the crossing between Asia and Europe was easiest. Istanbul began as a humble fishing village, but because it straddled two continents and had a deep, sheltered harbor, it became the seat of empires and a crossroads of the world.

Great cities don't just survive—they endure. Istanbul has had much to endure. The city has served as the capital of three empires (the Roman, Byzantine, and Ottoman Empires) and has lived through

Situated on a peninsula, Istanbul boasts picturesque views of the Blue Mosque *(left)* and the city skyline at sunset *(above)*. People relax in the shadow of the magnificent Bosporus Bridge *(right)*.

countless earthquakes, fires, and plagues. It has had three names—Byzantium, Constantinople, and Istanbul. For more than two millennia, the city beat back numerous invaders, including repeated attacks by Russian, Slavic, and Arab armies. But it has also been conquered by Persian kings and Roman emperors, European crusaders, and Ottoman Turks. In 2,600 years, this enduring city has grown from a tiny village to a metropolis of 12 million people.

A lively city, Istanbul mixes both ancient and modern worlds. Centuries-old markets sell everything from antique jewelry to athletic shoes. Modern hotels sit next to ancient mosques (Islamic houses of worship). Kids play soccer on what was once the floor of a church built more than 1,500 years ago. Peddlers, carrying huge loads on their backs as they've done for centuries, compete with noisy diesel trucks. Sixth-century Christian churches, converted to mosques, sport Islamic minarets (towers). Loudspeakers attached to these towers amplify the chant of the *muezzin* (prayer caller) summoning the devout. For centuries a target of foreign armies, Istanbul continues to surprise and delight modern "invaders"—visitors from the United States, Europe, and Asia.

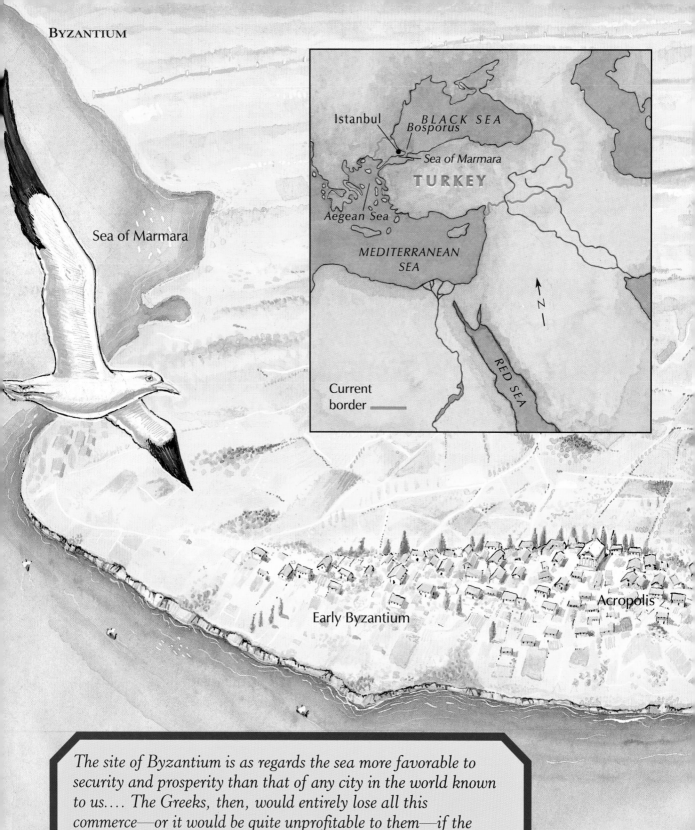

Sea of Marmara

Istanbul
Bosporus
BLACK SEA
Sea of Marmara
Aegean Sea
TURKEY
MEDITERRANEAN
SEA
RED SEA

Current
border ———

Early Byzantium

Acropolis

The site of Byzantium is as regards the sea more favorable to
security and prosperity than that of any city in the world known
to us…. The Greeks, then, would entirely lose all this
commerce—or it would be quite unprofitable to them—if the
Byzantines were disposed to be deliberately unfriendly to them.
—Polybius, second-century historian

Byzas and the Founding of Byzantium

In the thirteenth century B.C., settlers from Mycenae (ancient Greece) established a colony on the southwest end of the Bosporus—a narrow channel connecting the Black Sea and the Sea of Marmara. The colony eventually died out, and the acropolis (hillside fortress) that the colonists had built disappeared. But nearly 600 years later, Byzantium, a city named after its founder, Byzas, replaced the settlement on its exact site.

Byzas came from Megara, a Greek town located near Athens. With a band of fellow Greeks, he set sail in 657 B.C. to find new land. The oracle of Apollo, a famous Greek prophet, had advised Byzas to seek a new home "opposite to the land of the blind men." Byzas knew of no city populated by a majority of blind people, and he had only this confusing clue to help find a favorable site for a new village.

Upon reaching the Sea of Marmara where it meets the Bosporus, Byzas discovered the Golden Horn, a deep harbor sheltered from strong winds. A few years earlier, settlers from Megara had bypassed its protected waters in favor of a site on the opposite (Asian) side of the Bosporus. Byzas had his sign. The earlier settlers had not been physically blind but rather blind to the advantages of the site. By 600 B.C., the city-state of Byzantium surrounded a new acropolis and had walls protecting the city from invaders. An ancient historian dismissed it as "a feeble colony of Greeks." But Byzantium became the largest and richest of the Greek colonies on the Bosporus, collecting tolls from ships that passed through the strait. During many wars, the Persians as well as the Greek city-states of Sparta and Athens fought to control this strategic settlement.

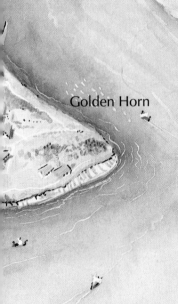

Golden Horn

Bosporus Strait

The Roman Conquest

Conquered by the Persian king Darius I in 512 B.C., Byzantium remained under Persian control until the Greeks retook it in 477 B.C. Fought over by Athens and Sparta, the city won its independence in 355 B.C. But by 129 B.C., Byzantium was paying tribute for its protection to the Republic of Rome. Emperor Vespasian incorporated Byzantium into the Roman Empire in A.D. 73, but the city remained free.

When Rome faced a war of imperial succession in 193, Byzantium backed Pescennius Niger, the rival of the Roman emperor Lucius Septimus Severus. For nearly three years, Severus's forces attacked Byzantium. Facing certain defeat, the Byzantines continued to defend themselves, heaving huge stones and bronze statues from their public buildings onto their attackers. The starving citizens resorted to cannibalism. To escape

Byzantium, they built ships from boards they stripped from their houses, and they braided ropes from the women's hair. A storm sank the overloaded ships, however. Severus then sacked the city and killed all the surviving soldiers and magistrates.

Severus's son, Marcus Aurelius Antoninus, persuaded the emperor to pardon the Byzantines, since their site was so valuable. Within five years, Severus rebuilt Byzantium and renamed it Antoninia after his son (although that name never caught on). The new city was more than twice the size of the original village that Byzas had founded.

Severus built public baths, a stadium, a forum, and a theater and amphitheater for wild animal shows and gladiator combat. The rebuilt city remained peaceful until 268, when the Visigoths, a Germanic group from northern Europe, tried to invade. Thanks to its new walls, the city repelled its attackers.

When they saw their friends perishing all together, the united throng set up a chorus of groans and lamentations, and after that they mourned for the rest of the day and the whole night…. The next day the horror was increased still more for the townspeople. For when the water had subsided, the whole sea in the vicinity of Byzantium was covered with corpses and wrecks and blood, and many of the remains were cast up on shore.

—Dio Cassius, second-century Roman senator and historian

9

Constantine the Great

By the third century, the Roman Empire was so large that it needed two emperors. But the system of shared rule soon collapsed. In 324 Constantine—ruler of the empire's western provinces—defeated the eastern emperor Licinius to become sole ruler of the Roman Empire. Recognizing the strategic setting of Byzantium near the empire's eastern provinces, Constantine rebuilt the city as Nova Roma (New Rome), the new capital of the Roman Empire. But the city soon became known as Constantinople, after its ruler.

Constantine founded a city that would serve as the center of the world. He established schools to train artisans and architects. He imported columns and statues from ancient Greek and Asian cities and built forums and villas. Within four years, the city's public buildings began to rival those of Rome. Within a century, Constantinople became the most populous city in the world.

Had Constantine done nothing but build a magnificent new capital, he would have secured a place in history. But Constantine was the first Roman emperor to embrace Christianity, a religion that was gaining popularity within the empire. Previously, Roman emperors had been the head of a pagan religion with many gods. They had persecuted people who held Christian beliefs. But before a crucial battle in 312, Constantine had a vision of a cross (the symbol of Christianity) in the sky. The cross bore a banner urging him to conquer under that sign. Inspired by this vision, he stopped the persecution of Christians. On his deathbed, he was baptized into the Christian faith.

While Constantine did not make Christianity the empire's official religion, he saw himself as head of that religion. He envisioned Constantinople as the new capital of a Christian empire. At the time, Christians made up only about 25 percent of the Roman Empire's population, but they were steadily gaining converts.

In this tapestry, the Roman emperor Constantine meets with his city planners to design his grand new capital.

Walls of Theodosius

Alarmed by the capture of Rome by the Visigoths in 410, Emperor Theodosius II ordered that new walls be built to protect Constantinople from land invasion. The city had outgrown the walls that Constantine erected. Everyone had to help, either with money or labor. Stretching for four miles, the walls established Constantinople's western boundaries. Connecting to the seawalls that protected the shoreline, the new walls completely enclosed the city.

In 447 earthquakes crumbled the walls, but they were rebuilt in less than two months. A moat (water-filled trench) was added and a new outer wall built—just in time to convince hordes of nomadic Huns (Central Asian invaders led by Attila the Hun) to direct their attacks elsewhere. The walls protected Constantinople from Persian, Arab, and Russian armies.

Ballista

Onager

The people of Constantinople were experts at building walls, and the walls of Theodosius proved one of the most remarkable fortifications ever built. Attackers first met a 60-foot-wide, 15-foot-deep moat. After crossing the moat, they faced an outer rampart (barrier) that rose higher than 200 feet from the bottom of the moat. Warriors who scaled it were hit with stones, spears, and boiling oil. Next came a second wall, over which loomed 96 huge towers. This middle wall was followed by a third wall that was 40 feet high and defended by 96 more towers. From these towers—each 70 feet high—soldiers repelled invaders with arrows or enormous stones that they heaved with catapult machines known as onagers. Ingenious as the fortifications were, it took a lot of men to defend them.

After the fall of Rome in 476, the Western Roman Empire was carved into smaller kingdoms. Constantinople remained the capital of the Eastern Roman Empire, to which modern scholars refer as the Byzantine Empire.

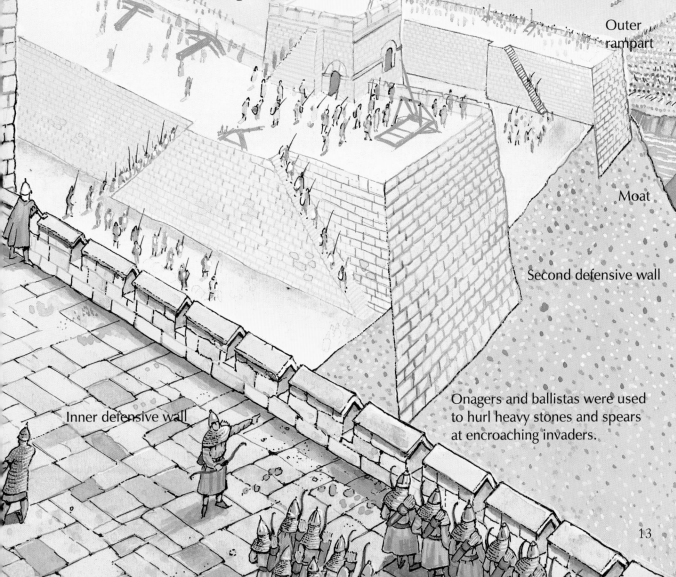

Outer rampart

Moat

Second defensive wall

Onagers and ballistas were used to hurl heavy stones and spears at encroaching invaders.

Inner defensive wall

Justinian

Born a peasant in what would become Yugoslavia, Flavius Petrus Sabbatius became one of the most famous emperors of all time. Renamed Justinian I, he ruled the Byzantine Empire from 527 to 565. He prayed that God would allow him to recapture the lands of the old Roman Empire "which have been lost through indolence." Reconquering Italy, parts of Spain, and Africa's northern coast, Justinian nearly restored the Roman Empire to its most extensive ancient boundaries.

Justinian was equally famed for his achievements in Constantinople. Under him the city became grander than ever. The art and architecture he sponsored were refreshingly different from Roman styles. And Constantinople became one of the leading commercial centers of the world.

Roman emperors had always been builders, and Justinian wanted to erect monuments worthy of his name. For rich citizens of Constantinople, this meant additional taxes—which they paid, but about which they complained. Justinian was also concerned about the welfare of the people. He built hospitals for and offered free medical care to the city's many poor residents. The empire's social welfare programs ensured that no one went hungry. Twenty state bakeries gave free bread to anyone who needed it, and the public baths were free to all residents.

In perhaps his most significant act, Justinian compiled all Roman laws (more than 4,600 of them)—a massive undertaking. Outdated laws were dropped. Some of the new laws guaranteed the rights of widows and championed the rights of slaves over masters and wives over husbands. Justinian's legal code defined the relationship between the people and the government according to Roman tradition. The new body of laws also incorporated certain Christian beliefs. The territories he won, the buildings he erected, and the law system he reformed make Justinian one of the greatest rulers of all time.

These mosaics depict Empress Theodora with her court *(left)* and her husband, Emperor Justinian I *(above)*—a leader so busy and concerned for the welfare of his people that he was known as the emperor who never slept.

Home and Public Life

During the reign of Justinian, Constantinople boasted a population of six hundred thousand. The city included people of Greek and Roman descent as well as Egyptians, Armenians, Franks, Celts, Illyrians, and Huns. Constantinople also regularly welcomed merchants and visitors from distant lands. Although citizens of Constantinople considered themselves Roman, most spoke Greek. To be a citizen of Constantinople, an individual had to belong to the Christian Church and be able to speak Greek.

Modest and poor homes might lie right next to the homes of the rich. Most wealthier houses were two stories or higher. They were built of brick around a central courtyard containing a fountain or a garden with ornamental trees. Only the upper floors, many of them fitted with balconies, had windows. Strict regulations made sure that no house cut off a wealthy neighbor's light or view of the sea.

Ordinary working people were crammed into small houses with dirt floors or into tenements as tall as 10 stories. The poor built squatters' shacks in slums, where theft and murder were common.

Constantinople's narrow, twisting streets were crowded with pedestrians and animals. Often the streets were too narrow for carts. Porters had to carry goods within parts of the city.

The roles of men and women were clearly defined. Wealthy men served in the government and owned land. There was also a professional class of engineers, physicians, and architects. The working class consisted of merchants and artisans. Women played a secondary role in public life. They rarely left their homes except to go to church or to the public baths. They were banned from sporting events and attended church in a separate section from the men. They wore veils outside and when receiving male guests in their homes. Other than family members and certain slaves, no men were allowed into their quarters. Despite such social restrictions, the status of women improved under the Christian Church, which banned divorce and supported widows and orphans.

Homes of the wealthy all had clear views of the sea.

Constantinople was a city of grand palaces and impressive public buildings. A main thoroughfare called the Mese (Middle Way) connected the palace area and government buildings at the eastern end of the city with the western end. The Mese was flanked on both sides by a covered colonnade housing shops, booths, and cafes. The street was the site of much commercial and social activity.

Women were secluded inside their homes. When they went out, they were required to wear a veil.

Wealthy families enjoyed the service of household slaves who helped the children wash and dress.

The Hippodrome

From hosting displays of wild animals, political meetings, and religious rituals to offering shelter from the city's recurrent earthquakes, the Hippodrome was the hub of social life in Constantinople. An emperor once delayed the news of an approaching army lest he spoil the fun in the Hippodrome.

The most popular event was the chariot races. Nearly eighty thousand spectators regularly packed the stands to cheer and bet on their favorite charioteers. Sports clubs called the Blues and the Greens organized the events and supported opposing racers. These clubs also supervised the halftime entertainment. Acrobats, clowns, and musicians performed between as many as 24 chariot races a day.

The aristocratic Blues and lower-class Greens were politically powerful. Riots were common at the Hippodrome—often with disastrous consequences for the city's leaders. Many magistrates and several emperors lost their offices—even their lives—in the Hippodrome. Others came to power by courting the crowds who flocked there. Nowhere in Constantinople was the voice of the people louder than in the Hippodrome.

In 532 some Greens in the Hippodrome shouted insults at Emperor Justinian when he refused to spare members of their group who were to be executed for rioting. When he tried to silence the hecklers, the Blues and Greens united against him. For nine days, mobs shouting *Nika!* ("Victory!") destroyed public buildings. They even tried to burn down the Imperial Palace. Justinian had a ship readied for his escape, but his wife Theodora refused to leave. Strengthened by her willingness to face death over disgrace, Justinian ordered Belisarius, his most able general, to put down the revolt. With a small army, Belisarius blocked the exits to the Hippodrome, where the rioters were celebrating. The soldiers slaughtered thirty thousand rebels, most of them Greens. The Nika Revolt was over.

In this stone relief *(left)*, Emperor Theodosius I presides over games at the Hippodrome. In later years, the Hippodrome fell into disuse but remained a public meeting place and home to an Egyptian obelisk *(below)*.

That one who has been emperor should become an exile I cannot bear.... If you wish safety, my lord, that is an easy matter. We are rich, and there is the sea, and yonder our ships. But consider whether, if you reach safety, you may not desire to exchange that safety for death. As for me, I like the old saying that the purple is the noblest shroud.

—Theodora's words to Justinian, as recorded by the historian Procopius

Hagia Sophia

Much of Constantinople's public life centered on the church. In addition to elaborate ceremonies in churches, there were many public processions and celebrations to honor holy days. The city's main church was Hagia Sophia (Holy Wisdom), which Constantine had begun and his son Constantius had finished. Burned down by rioters, its replacement, built in 415, was also destroyed. Justinian immediately planned a new church on its site. He did more than pay for it.

According to a historian of his time, he "assisted at its building by the labor and powers of his mind."

Although Justinian built 25 new churches during his reign, Hagia Sophia would become the greatest church of the city and the empire. Justinian hired the best mathematicians he could find—Anthemius of Tralles and Isidorus of Miletus—to be his principal architects. In less than six years, ten thousand workers—mostly slaves under the direction of a hundred foremen—created an architectural marvel. Hundreds

> *Glory to God, who has thought me worthy to finish this work. Solomon, I have outdone you!*
> —Emperor Justinian at the completion of Hagia Sophia in 537, comparing it to King Solomon's temple in Jerusalem

of stonemasons, sculptors, mosaicists, carpenters, bricklayers, and plasterers worked overtime on the gigantic project. Laborers used shiploads of richly veined marble to fashion the church's elaborate interior. Four acres of gold-backed stones formed mosaics that adorned the ceilings. Cascading domes led to a central dome 18 stories high, providing a sense of vastness and light.

The cost of the new church was staggering, and not just to Justinian's treasury. Some city officials went unpaid

and some schools remained empty to help defray the construction costs of the enormous project. For a thousand years, Hagia Sophia was the largest enclosed human-made space on earth. Although earthquakes shook its foundations, the glorious church lived on.

Over time Byzantine churches began to practice Christianity differently than Roman churches did. The western churches became Roman Catholic, while those in Constantinople became Eastern Orthodox.

From the time of Constantine, artists in Constantinople were exempt from all forms of public service on the condition that they devote all their time to perfecting their craft and passing their skills on to their sons.

Mosaic icons like this famous image of Jesus *(above)* were focal points in Constantinople's churches. Mosaics depicting animals, like the humped bull *(right)* and coiled fish *(facing page)* often decorated homes and public buildings.

Mosaic Art

An icon is an image, usually depicting religious figures and holy persons, on small wooden panels or on church walls. Icons were considered an important element of Christian worship in Constantinople. They appeared in the form of paintings or mosaics—pictures made from tiny bits of colored stone and glass. Mosaics became the major art form of the Byzantine Empire in the sixth century, and the churches of Constantinople were famous for their dazzling mosaics. Depicting the life of Jesus and of various Christian saints, these works appeared on church walls, floors, and ceilings. Some people had mosaics in their homes, too.

The city gave its artists special status. They were free from public service so long as they practiced and taught their craft to an apprentice.

A mosaic apprentice, working under a master, first learned how to crush stones and cut colored glass rods into small pieces called tesserae. Some tesserae were as small as a match head. Next the apprentice helped to cover a wall with a smooth layer of plaster. A design was then sketched on the wall. Finally a finishing coat of plaster had to be applied. While the finishing plaster was still wet, the apprentice learned to press the tesserae into place quickly and carefully. At first he would be given only background work—a solid color to set off a central mosaic figure. After a while, the mosaicist would allow his apprentice to do part of a figure—a piece of a robe, or the wings of an angel. The master showed him how to angle the tesserae so they would scatter the light of the church candles and make the figures glow. It was slow, exacting work. After two years, the apprentice might become a journeyman and a member of the mosaic guild, a kind of workers' union.

Education

Education was widespread among the people of Constantinople. The city's first schools were church schools for boys training to become priests. Saint Basil, the fourth-century founder of the first monastery, wanted all children admitted to such schools. This was forbidden later, however, by a church council in 451. Yet in wealthy homes, monks often tutored children. From the time of Justinian onward, the church was no longer the exclusive provider of education. Schooling became available for many children.

In their homes, mothers taught their children to read. Then, at the age of five, children went to school. Instructors taught in Greek, the language that people spoke every day. Students learned grammar (including reading and writing), then advanced grammar and ancient Greek classics. Children were expected to memorize 50 lines of the *Iliad*, a famous Greek epic poem, every day. Sons of the very rich received schooling at home. Their tutors had permission to beat idle pupils.

At the age of 14, most boys went to secondary school, where they studied oratory (public speaking) and classic Greek writers such as Demosthenes. They also studied philosophy, arithmetic, geometry, music, and astronomy. The sciences were considered less important than theoretical and philosophical subjects. The secondary school functioned as a combination high school and college, and students stayed for six years or more. Some young people went on to advanced study in law school. But for many professions, such as medicine, training was accomplished by apprenticeship.

Girls were not as well educated as boys were. At home they might share lessons with their brothers or might have their own tutor. But they could not enter a school or university. From the age of 10, most girls were instructed only in skills such as sewing and cooking, which they would need to run a household. But some daughters of wealthy parents managed to obtain an education comparable to that of their brothers.

Education in Constantinople—and throughout the empire—was based on classical Greek teachings. In this fourteenth-century illumination *(facing page, above)*, students gather to study philosophy at a school in Constantinople. Although only boys *(facing page, below)* could go to school, a girl whose parents could afford a tutor might follow all the studies that a boy would pursue at school.

There you could see a Latin furthering his education, a Scyth learning Greek, a Roman handling Greek texts, an illiterate Greek learning how to read his own language.

—Anna Comnena, describing a grammar school for orphans founded in Constantinople by her father, Alexius I, in the eleventh century

25

The Iconoclasts

For much of the Byzantine Empire's history, the throne belonged to anyone who could gain and keep it. Even when hereditary succession became common, the people could oust a ruler by violent protests. Almost half of Constantinople's 88 emperors were forced out. Thirteen were banished, eight were blinded, and twenty-one were murdered.

In 641 the emperor Heraclius tried to name his wife Marino coruler with his young son, but the people were against it. When Marino tried to defy them, her stepson had her tongue cut out and took the throne himself. Only three women ruled the empire on their own. The first of these, Irene, had her own son's eyes gouged out so she could succeed him as emperor. A former stable boy became Emperor Basil I when he murdered the ruler who had befriended him. The Byzantine Empire's history of plots and violence often overshadows its achievements.

One of the biggest conflicts in the history of Constantinople dealt with religion—a topic about which the city was passionate. Byzantine emperors led church councils that clarified Christian

Iconoclasts destroy religious icons while mosaic artists are led to prison in chains.

doctrine. Religious debate was followed as closely as sporting events. As early as the fourth century, Saint Gregory of Nyssa discovered that even the city's bakers and bath attendants eagerly offered their views on complex theological issues. Constantinople's soldiers carried sacred Christian relics and icons into battle, shouting "the cross has conquered" when they attacked an enemy.

A religious controversy erupted in 730 when Emperor Leo III ordered all icons portraying God, Jesus, or the saints destroyed. Leo thought icons could foster the worship of images.

Iconoclasts (image breakers) destroyed beautiful mosaics throughout Constantinople. They imprisoned or executed hundreds of people who tried to defend the artworks. Leo III limited mosaic artists to decorating churches with plain crosses or figures of animals and plants—not human beings.

Finally, in 845, a church council in Constantinople restored the right to the popular practice of honoring icons. Mosaic art once again flourished within the city. To this day, the Orthodox Church celebrates this decision with an annual festival.

O city, city, eye of all cities, known throughout the world and a sight for all, mother of churches, leader of religion…guardian of letters and all that is lovely, bitterly have you drunk from the cup of the Lord's anger.

—Nicetas Choniates, Byzantine government official and historian

Soldiers from the Fourth Crusade ransacked and profaned Constantinople, burning entire sections of the city and shipping countless art treasures and sacred relics to France and Italy.

The Crusades

Since its founding, Constantinople had been repeatedly besieged by invading armies. But no attack was more damaging than that of the knights of the Fourth Crusade. The Crusades were armed religious pilgrimages authorized by the pope (the leader of the Roman Catholic Church). Crusaders aimed to recapture Jerusalem for the Christian faith after Islamic armies took that city in 1071. Jerusalem was important to Christians because it was the city where Jesus had lived and died. Crusaders took the city in 1096, but Islamic forces later retook it. In 1203 Pope Innocent III commissioned the Fourth Crusade to conquer Jerusalem once again. The city-state of Venice, an important commercial center and the Mediterranean's largest sea power at the time, agreed to support the venture. On their way to Jerusalem, the crusaders launched a surprise attack on Constantinople, Venice's rival in trade. The young Alexius IV, whose father, Isaac, had been removed as Byzantine emperor and blinded by his own brother Alexius III, had promised financial support to the crusaders if they helped remove his rival from the throne. He had also promised to place the empire under the religious domination of the pope.

On June 23, 1203, the ships of the Fourth Crusade arrived, bearing thirty thousand troops. Because many citizens supported Alexius IV, there was no all-out resistance to the siege. In a little over a month, the city was taken for the first time in nine hundred years. That mission accomplished, the crusaders should have gone on to Jerusalem. But the newly installed Emperor Alexius IV couldn't pay the crusaders as much as he had promised, and they refused to leave without their reward. Eventually, the citizens of Constantinople turned against the emperor and the occupiers. On April 12, 1204, the crusaders sacked the city, slaughtering two thousand residents.

For more than half a century, the crusaders ruled the city until the Greeks took it in 1261. After its capture, Constantinople lost much of its glory. The Fourth Crusade became known as the Unholy Crusade.

Conquest

In the fourteenth century, the weakened Byzantine Empire and its capital city became a target for the Ottoman Turks. Originally nomads from Central Asia, the Turks developed a common culture and language after the eighth century. By the end of the tenth century, most Turks had converted to Islam, the religion founded by the prophet Muhammad in the seventh century. In the eleventh century, under Seljuk, the Turks settled in Anatolia, modern Turkey's central plain. After the Seljuk kingdom died out, a leader named Osman became dominant and founded the Osmanli (Ottoman) dynasty.

Mehmed II, the sultan (ruler) of the Ottomans, saw Constantinople as a gateway to Europe. Expecting an attack from Mehmed's forces, Emperor Constantine XI turned to Rome for help in 1451. But since 1054, the Eastern Orthodox and the Roman Catholic Churches had been divided over the issue of church leadership. Rome promised aid to Constantinople if the emperor agreed to accept the pope as supreme authority in church matters. Constantine agreed, but many in the city blamed the pope for the Fourth Crusade and refused to accept the terms. Many felt they would be freer to practice their form of Christianity under a sultan than under a pope.

In March of 1453, Mehmed II launched a massive assault on the city with 20,000 men and 493 ships. Constantinople had only about 5,000 men, plus nearly 3,000 Italian allies, to defend itself. The Turks aimed the largest cannon in the world at the city walls. Each night the defenders rebuilt the walls with dirt and wood. A huge length of iron chain kept the Turkish ships from entering the Golden Horn. But Mehmed engineered an ingenious way around this. He had teams of oxen drag 70 ships uphill over a road of oiled logs and planks and down into the Golden Horn, allowing the Turks to take control of the harbor. The siege continued for more than seven weeks. Finally Turkish troops poured through a breach in the walls. Mehmed II became known as Mehmed the Conqueror. With the conquest of the city and the death of Constantine XI, the Byzantine Empire officially ended.

Ottoman forces pitch camp outside Constantinople (above) and later celebrate their conquest of the city (facing page).

Better the sultan's turban than the cardinal's hat.
—Lucas Notarus, last grand admiral of the Byzantine navy

Refuge of the World

After his conquest of the city, Mehmed II made Constantinople the capital of the Ottoman Empire and a holy city of Islam.

For his new capital, Mehmed II required a world-class city, which Constantinople was not. From six hundred thousand residents in the sixth century, it was down to thirty thousand. Mehmed needed a large population to serve the palace and the state.

The largest group of people Mehmed imported were Turks from Anatolia. He also brought in many Christian residents from provinces that the empire had conquered. Although it was the capital of an Islamic empire, non-Muslims made up 40 percent of the city Mehmed repopulated. Housed in separate neighborhoods, Christians lived the same modest lifestyle as Muslim city residents. Unlike their Muslim neighbors, however, they had to pay a tax to the sultan.

Mehmed II's court always bustled with fascinating guests from around the world. He was the first sultan to invite European artists into his court.

To bring people to the city, Mehmed relied on *devshirme* (the collecting), a practice begun by his father. Recruiting parties went to villages in captive regions, such as Greece, and chose Christian males between the ages of 8 and 20. Although forcible conversion was not usual in Islam, those "collected" were converted to the religion to make sure they would have no loyalties that might conflict with their faithfulness to the sultan. Some families accepted recruitment because it meant that the emperor would provide for their sons. Others hid their children or arranged child marriages to make their sons ineligible for recruitment. After training and schooling, those boys most suited for the military became Janissaries (soldiers). The rest served as pages, policemen, or gardeners.

Christians were free to practice their religion and worship in churches as long as they agreed not to ring the church bells. Constantinople also had many Jewish residents.

Like many of the city rulers that preceded him, Mehmed was a builder. He had public buildings, marketplaces, and mosques constructed around the city. He even had Hagia Sophia converted into a mosque. Though known as the Conqueror, Mehmed saw himself as the Helper. He built a huge mosque where he fed a thousand people a day.

At Mehmed's death in 1481, the city's population had grown to eighty thousand residents. Some 18 nationalities coexisted in the city—the only multinational European capital of its day. Mehmed called the city Refuge of the World. Although Constantinople was not officially renamed until 1930, the city came to be known as Istanbul. The name derives from a Greek phrase that means "into the city."

A Golden Era

From his court in Istanbul, Süleyman I reigned from 1520 to 1566 over the most powerful empire in the world. At the age of 25, he became sultan and soon advanced the borders of the Ottoman Empire farther than any other sultan had. His forces captured much of the North African coast, defeated Hungary, and conquered the city of Baghdad.

Süleyman presided over a golden era in the history of the Ottoman Empire and of the city. He attended mosque services every Friday in a magnificent procession accompanied by hundreds of attendants. Dressed in splendid robes, he rode a white horse whose saddle was studded with precious gems. Astounded at the splendor of his court, Europeans gave him the title Süleyman the Magnificent.

Like the Christian emperor Justinian in the same city a thousand years earlier, Süleyman was known not just for military triumphs or for splendor. He earned fame for domestic policies and programs, as well as for his interpretation of holy law based on the Koran (the holy book of Islam). Fines, which were heavier for the rich than for the poor, replaced capital punishment as the penalty for many crimes. Süleyman ensured equal treatment for all Muslim subjects and reduced the special tax that non-Muslims had to pay. For systematizing the laws and eliminating many abuses, he earned the title Süleyman the Lawgiver.

Like many sultans, Süleyman was highly cultured. His staff included 30 painters and 100 calligraphers. A poet himself, he generously supported the arts. He employed dozens of artists in his palace. He also ordered the building of many new mosques and had his architects rebuild the city's aqueducts and water towers, ensuring a sufficient supply of freshwater.

Süleyman the Magnificent tours the ruins of the Hippodrome (facing page). He often adorned himself in a turban topped with peacock feathers and diamonds (facing page, inset). Süleyman's court (above) celebrates the circumcision of a royal prince.

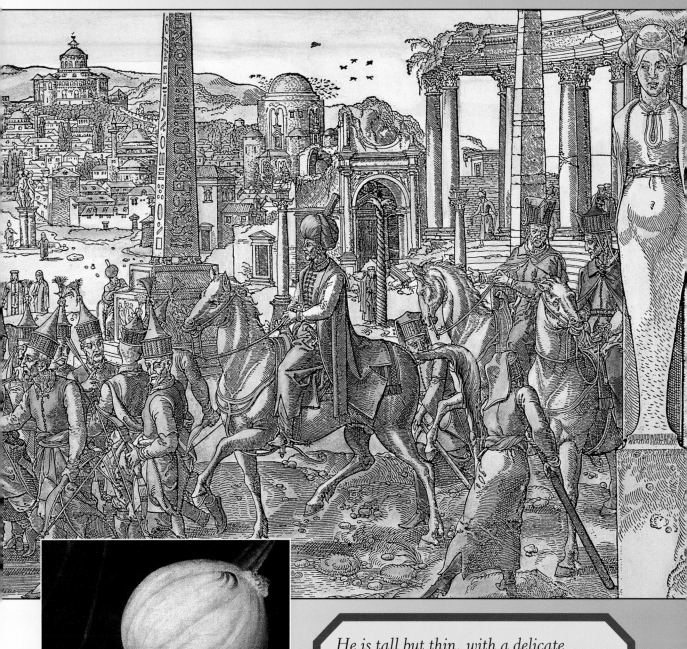

He is tall but thin, with a delicate complexion. His nose is a little too long, his features fine, and his nose aquiline. He has the shadow of a moustache and a short beard. His general appearance is pleasing, although he is a little pale.

—Venetian ambassador Bartolomeo Contarini describing Süleyman when he took office at the age of 25

35

A Time of Building

As a young man, the architect Sinan was taken from his village in Turkey by an Ottoman recruiting party and converted from Christianity to Islam. He had built only bridges and barracks for the army when Süleyman made him his chief architect around 1538. Already in his forties, Sinan would live to serve three sultans over fifty years, creating more than three hundred structures in Turkey. He built 42 large mosques in Istanbul alone. At the age of 66 he finished one of his greatest works, al-Süleymaniye (Süleyman's mosque), the finest of the city's Ottoman buildings.

Al-Süleymaniye loomed larger than Hagia Sophia, dominating the city's skyline. Each of its four minarets had 10 galleries to honor Süleyman, the tenth Ottoman sultan. As many as 250 muezzins could climb those towers to chant the daily calls to prayer. An enormous central dome set on four pillars made the interior much lighter and more open than other Istanbul mosques. For evening worship, hundreds of oil lamps hung on a circle of chains suspended from the ceiling. To create the lamps, glassblowers had shaped molten glass fired in a furnace. From a gallery Sinan designed, lamplighters lit the lamps. Like other imperial mosques, al-Süleymaniye also included a soup kitchen, a school, and baths.

The mosque complex took seven years to complete. More than 3,500 laborers worked on the project. Stone carvers and wood-carvers created the mosque's doors, windows, and screens. Scores of metalworkers and glassworkers created the stained glass windows. Artisans painted and fired hundreds of tiles with intricate designs in bright colors. Although women were not allowed to work on the mosque, women and children made the carpets that covered the floor on which worshipers prayed.

Mosques were a central part of life in Istanbul, a city devoted to Islam. No city had more mosques. Their main purpose was to serve as a place of worship. But they also played an important role in education. Students at mosque schools earned a traditional Islamic education, which combined religious studies with the arts and sciences. In addition, some mosques included inns and hospitals.

Prayer was a central part of life for Istanbul's Muslim residents. Five times a day, the muezzins would call people to prayer. Inside the city's mosques, worshipers knelt on handmade rugs to pray. Before entering a mosque, worshipers would wash their faces, hands, arms, and feet in a fountain outside.

Life in the Capital City

Visitors to Istanbul often remarked on the breathtaking view of the city as seen from the 220-foot-high Galata Tower—which was built in 1348—across the Golden Horn. Majestic ships and small boats filled the harbor. Palaces and large wooden homes called *yalis* lined the shores of the city. Away from the shore, tightly packed wooden houses ran along narrow, winding streets. Among these homes were mosques, public buildings, and gardens.

Homes of the rich had large reception rooms decorated with Persian carpets, jewels, and rich fabrics. Ordinary homes were smaller, with two to four rooms. Most Ottoman houses had little furniture. Beds were stored in cupboards and rolled out onto the floor at night.

A common destination for the men of the city was the coffeehouse. Coffee was introduced to Istanbul during the sixteenth century, and the first coffeehouse opened in 1554. Coffeehouses soon became an important part of male social life. Women in Istanbul were mostly confined to the home and to household duties. At least once a week, however, women would gather in the city's public baths to bathe, relax, and meet with friends.

At the juncture of the Bosporus, the Sea of Marmara, and the Golden Horn lay

Topkapi Palace, the jewel of the city. *Topkapi* means "cannon gate"—a name that emphasized the fortress that the palace was. Many gates guarded a compound of residences, libraries, audience rooms, summer homes, kitchens, and gardens. The palace walls enclosed not only the sultanate but also the judiciary and the military. Four courtyards enclosed the largest palace grounds in Europe. Five thousand people once lived in this town within a town.

By the eighteenth century, Istanbul was a stunning port city (*above*).

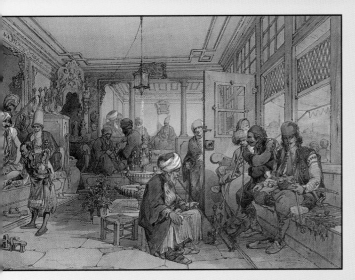

Coffeehouses were a center of social life for men. They would sit for hours drinking coffee, chatting, smoking, and playing games.

Topkapi Palace was often a violent place. Over the outside gates, severed heads of executed persons were thrust on spikes. Inside, scores of young princes were strangled on the orders of their fathers or uncles. This savage practice ensured that the young men could never grow up to challenge the power of a ruling sultan.

From 1617 onward, the brothers of a ruling sultan were confined to a few small rooms and forbidden to marry or have children. On the death of a sultan, only the one next in line was released. Princes who came to the throne after years in seclusion were poorly equipped to rule an empire. But more than 20 of them did so.

Guilds and Merchants

Because of the size of Istanbul's port and its location at the crossroads of Europe and Asia, the city was a thriving center of commerce. Trading ships filled Istanbul's harbor, the Golden Horn, and the city's markets overflowed with goods from around the Ottoman Empire and beyond. Because of the city's brisk commerce, the population rose steadily. Foreign merchants flocked to Istanbul to make their fortune.

The most important item of trade was food. Warehouses along the Golden Horn were well stocked with spices from Egypt, meat from the Balkans and Anatolia, and fruit from the imperial lands along the Black Sea. The Bosporus, the Sea of Marmara, and the Black Sea provided plentiful amounts of fish. With food flowing in from all parts of the world, Istanbul rarely suffered from food shortages.

At the center of the city's commercial life were guilds, or professional organizations, formed by merchants or members of a particular trade. The guilds in Istanbul regulated competition within a trade and obtained common privileges for their members. During the 1500s and 1600s, more than a thousand guilds operated in Istanbul. There were guilds for bakers, butchers, carpenters—even thieves! Guilds regulated commercial activity in Istanbul and also served a social purpose, providing an identity for members. In addition, guilds founded mutual aid societies that fed the poor and secured jobs for unemployed members. Most guilds cut across religious lines to include Muslim, Christian, and Jewish members. But competition between guilds for members could be intense, sometimes leading to rivalries and fights.

The market was a bustling and crowded center of commerce, rich in the great variety of goods that arrived at the port of Istanbul.

Slavery

By 1600 one out of five people in Istanbul was a slave. Many were prisoners of war. Boys and young men were also collected from nations under the empire. In the Ottoman Empire, one-fifth of all slaves went to the sultan. Most male slaves served in the army or at the sultan's court. Women and girls were bought for the sultan's harem or used as domestic servants. Some served as ladies-in-waiting to the chief women of the court. Wealthier families also owned slaves for domestic purposes.

Traders sold men, women, and children as young as three at Istanbul's slave market. Dealers usually displayed the men naked and forced the women to take a physical examination. The Istanbul slave market sold twenty thousand slaves every year. No one class or race was singled out for this unfortunate status. People from all over the empire were enslaved. Islamic law did not permit Turkish Muslims to be taken as slaves, however.

Ottoman slaves did have certain privileges. They could petition to be resold if their masters abused them. Some were allowed to own property. Many bought or earned their freedom through marriage. Slaves could even rise to a higher rank on their own merits. All of Süleyman's grand viziers (chief ministers) were Christian slaves converted to Islam. Nevertheless, slaves had very restricted rights and were considered property.

A slave woman who bore a sultan a son was given special treatment and better lodging. When such a son became sultan, his slave mother would become the most powerful woman in the Ottoman Empire. The Greek slave Kösem earned this distinction when her son Murad IV became sultan.

Customers examine slaves on display in Istanbul's slave bazaar. Many slaves were treated like livestock. Customers rubbed spit on slaves' faces to find out if make-up had been used to make them look healthier.

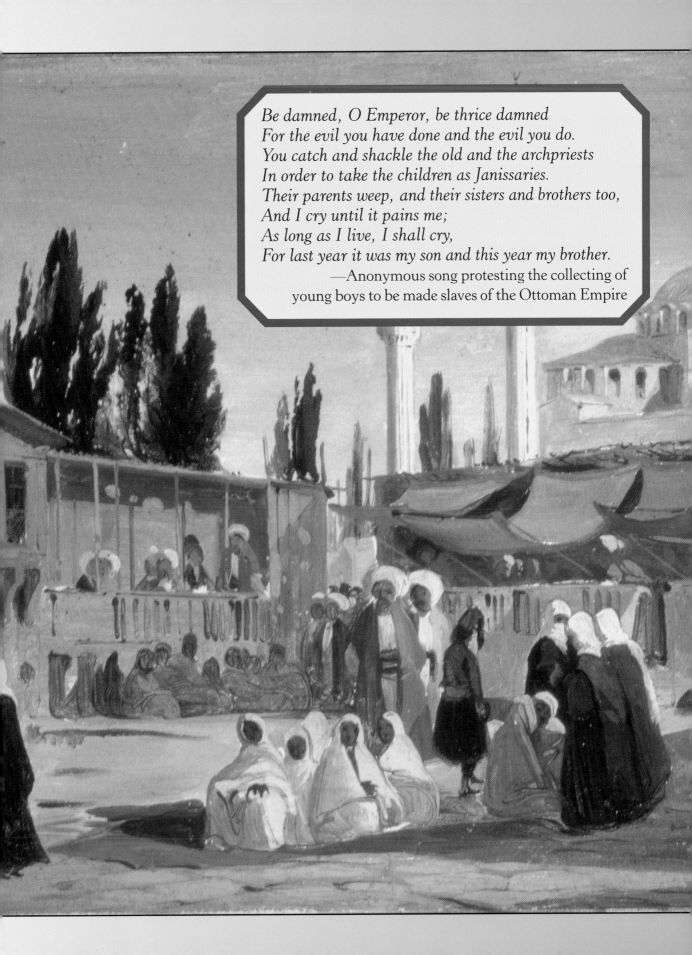

Be damned, O Emperor, be thrice damned
For the evil you have done and the evil you do.
You catch and shackle the old and the archpriests
In order to take the children as Janissaries.
Their parents weep, and their sisters and brothers too,
And I cry until it pains me;
As long as I live, I shall cry,
For last year it was my son and this year my brother.
　　　　—Anonymous song protesting the collecting of
　　　　young boys to be made slaves of the Ottoman Empire

The Police of Istanbul

Janissaries were the highly trained professional soldiers who policed Istanbul and served as the city's first fire brigades. Murad I, the third Ottoman sultan, created the elite fighting force in the late fourteenth century. Janissaries were a legion of young Christian men taken from Greece, Hungary, and other captive countries, converted to Islam, and taught the fundamentals of warfare. They were loyal to no one but the sultan.

After special training and education, the recruits most suited for the infantry were fitted with splendid uniforms topped with a huge cap that looked like an enormous folded sleeve. Forbidden to marry, the Janissaries were a highly religious, disciplined military fraternity. Well-fed and well-paid, they carried enormous brass soup pots—even into battle. In wartime a large contingent of Janissaries served as the Palace Guard, protecting the sultan in Istanbul's Topkapi Palace.

There were no more than a thousand Janissaries in the fourteenth century. But the force grew when married men and the

sons of ordinary tradesmen were admitted. Two centuries later, the ranks of the Janissaries had grown to 48,000 and were made up mostly of Muslim Turks. The Janissaries grew quite powerful—and if not properly paid, they even challenged the sultans they were sworn to serve. By the seventeenth century, they controlled Istanbul, killing government ministers. In 1622 they assassinated the teenaged sultan Osman II. Sultans could no longer rule without the Janissaries' support. Though once highly religious and well-disciplined, they became a corrupt band that terrorized Istanbul.

By the early nineteenth century, the Janissaries were no longer an effective fighting force. Accustomed to hand-to-hand combat, the troops refused to learn new ways of fighting. When they marched on the palace of Sultan Mahmud II to protest his reforms, forces loyal to the sultan opened fire. Six thousand Janissaries were killed. On the following day, May 1, 1826, Mahmud II exiled five thousand remaining Janissaries and abolished the corps after more than four hundred years in existence. So elated were the citizens of Istanbul that the action became known as the Auspicious Event.

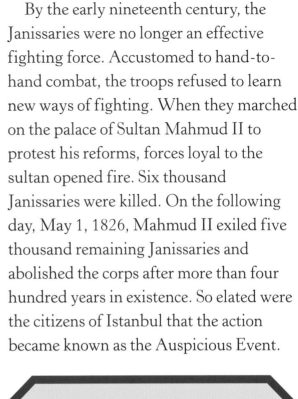

Their [the Janissaries'] discipline is far more just and strict than that of the ancient Greeks and Romans. There are three reasons for their superiority over us in battle: they immediately obey their commanders; they never worry about the possibility of losing their lives; and they can survive without bread and wine on a little barley and water.
—Paolo Giovio, Italian historian of the court of Süleyman, 1531

Türkisches Militär (Janitscharen).

A sultan inspects the ranks of his personal infantry, or Janissaries *(facing page)*. Janissaries carried curved swords and rifles or muskets *(left)*, although they believed that firearms could distract a soldier from his "natural warlike ardour." The word Janissary comes from *yeni çeri*, the Turkish words for "new troops."

There is a custom of the Turks to distinguish ranks by different turbans, as well as by fashion of dress, by the way of wearing sashes, and by the color of shoes, in public and private use.
—Luigi Fernandino Marsigli, eighteenth-century count and prisoner of the Turks

Ottoman Dress from Head to Toe

I n Ottoman Istanbul, men and women wore a caftan—a loose-fitting linen or silk robe that covered them to their ankles. In cold weather, men and women wore caftans lined with cotton or fur. Underneath their robes, men wore loose trousers plus a shirt and jacket with a wide sash. Attached to the trousers were soft leather socks, over which would go leather slippers or overshoes. Women wore baggy trousers and embroidered smocks topped with vests. Over leather socks they wore richly embroidered slippers, the toes of which came to a sharply upturned point. Wealthy women wore a lot of jewelry and a skullcap or bonnet decorated with pearls. Muslim women wore veils outside the home, in accordance with Islamic custom. Children dressed in the same style as their parents.

The Ottomans had rules that regulated dress. In the fifteenth century, Mehmed II regulated the color and cut of costumes for all officials. His advisers wore green, his chamberlains scarlet. Religious dignitaries wore purple. The distinctions were meant to signify rank. Similar rules also applied to the city's different religious and national groups. Christians and Jews were forbidden to dress like Muslims. Greeks wore sky blue skullcaps and black shoes. Armenians had dark blue (later red) caps and violet shoes. Jews wore yellow caps and blue slippers. All non-Muslim men wore dark robes. Even Istanbul's street sweepers had a distinctive costume—red leather smocks.

Only Muslim males could wear turbans—a single piece of cloth several yards long rolled around a felt cap covering a shaved head. Court officials wore their turbans around tall felt caps. Religious leaders had flatter turbans coiled around embroidered gold caps. Poor men wore simple, knotted pieces of cloth. The turbans of the wealthy were often decorated with sprays of diamonds.

In 1826 Sultan Mahmud II modernized court dress. A long black coat and European-style trousers were required as well as a fez—a red, conical cap. Only religious officials retained the turban and caftan. People protested Mahmud's rules but eventually accepted them in Istanbul and throughout the Ottoman Empire.

Muslim women in Constantinople wore veils that masked their faces from public view (facing page). The size of men's turbans was strictly regulated so that no man wore a turban that exceeded the height of the sultan's turban (inset).

47

Decline of the Empire

During the eighteenth and nineteenth centuries, the Ottoman Empire and its capital city underwent a gradual decline.

Continually at war to hold onto its far-flung territories, the empire eventually faced better-armed enemies. Clinging fiercely to old traditions that once earned conquests and glory, the empire failed to modernize its government and military. The Ottoman Empire became known as the Sick Man of Europe, and its neighbors waited for an opportunity to carve it up.

Sultan Abdülhamid II came to power in 1876, pledging to support a new constitution that would decrease the power of the sultanate. Instead he spent the next 30 years ruling with an iron fist. He used his secret police to crush all opposition. As a result, secret reform societies began popping up throughout Istanbul. In 1908 a group of soldiers called the Young Turks forced Abdülhamid II to restore the constitution. A year later, they removed the sultan and curtailed the powers of the sultanate. The citizens of Istanbul rejoiced.

But the problems of the empire and the city were not over. The Ottoman Empire sided with Germany in World War I (1914–1918) and was defeated. British, French, and Italian forces took over Istanbul—the city's first occupation by a foreign power since 1453. Foreign soldiers and refugees of the war crowded the city. To keep his throne, Sultan Mehmed VI went along with the Allies' plan for partitioning the empire. The Turkish residents of Istanbul, suffering from defeat and food shortages, were demoralized. But Greek and Armenian Christians, who had grown to resent their position as second-class citizens, found cause to celebrate.

Mustafa Kemal, a war hero, defied Mehmed VI and organized resistance to the foreign occupation. After winning a war of independence in 1922, Kemal abolished the sultanate the following year. The once glorious Ottoman Empire ended, and the Turkish Republic was born. As president of the new Turkish Republic, Kemal took the surname Atatürk (Father of the Turks).

The Allied forces divided the Ottoman Empire after its defeat in World War I. Turkish citizens endured the hardships of occupation and food shortages. Some resorted to begging in the streets.

Istanbul swells with images from past and present, from traditional foods *(below)* and clothing styles *(right)* to recurrent signs of an American and European presence *(facing page, left)*.

Between Two Worlds

As the first president of Turkey, Atatürk modernized the nation with sweeping reforms. He wanted the country to be more like the nations of Europe. Although Atatürk was not opposed to religion, he did not want it to interfere with government affairs. So Islam lost its standing as the official state religion, and religious schools closed. A code of civil laws replaced Islamic laws. The changes went beyond religion. The Latin alphabet replaced Arabic script. For the first time, all schools became coeducational (for both boys and girls).

Women were allowed to vote and were encouraged to remove their veils.

With the reforms of Atatürk, Istanbul's culture also changed. It became more secular (nonreligious) and lost much of its international flavor, as many Greek and Armenian residents left. Because the ethnic mix declined so severely, the city became overwhelmingly Turkish. Yet since this transformation, Istanbul has moved closer to adopting a European-style culture. Consciously, not just by geographic accident, it strives to be European.

Memorials throughout Turkey testify to the enormous respect Turks still hold for the accomplishments of their national hero, Atatürk (above).

Modern-day Istanbul embraces a number of contradictions. Alcohol, forbidden in many Muslim-majority cities, is readily available. In this city of believers and unbelievers, women wearing current fashions walk alongside women in all-concealing religious attire. Although a secular city, mosques and minarets still dominate the skyline. The government tries to keep religion out of politics, but many Muslims petition for extended rights over non-Muslims.

The city hopes to attract tourists, but it also wants to serve its residents—and both groups are growing. To attract visitors, Istanbul has opened new museums and has bulldozed squatters' shacks. But a thousand new residents arrive in the city every day, mostly from rural areas. These new arrivals live in modern concrete apartment towers that crowd the ancient city and its suburbs. As Istanbul expands and modernizes, it struggles to keep its identity.

When Atatürk moved Turkey's capital to Ankara in 1923, Istanbul was a city of eight hundred thousand. In 1999 Istanbul and its ever-expanding suburbs had 12 million residents. As at the height of the Byzantine and Ottoman Empires, Istanbul is again the most populated city in Europe.

Holidays and Special Events

Religious holidays and celebrations are important in Turkey. Each year Muslims observe the holy month of Ramadan, which is the ninth month of the Islamic lunar calendar. Muslims observe the month by fasting from dawn to dusk. Although many people in Istanbul keep the fast, visitors find that most restaurants and cafés stay open during the day.

Ramadan is followed by Seker Bayrami (the Sugar Festival), a joyous national holiday that marks the end of the fast. For three days, Turkish children go from door to door asking for sweets. People exchange cards and make visits. Travel is the main diversion. Businesses shut down, and public transportation in the city is free— if you can squeeze in, that is. Istanbul is ordinarily crowded, but when thousands of out-of-towners arrive at Seker Bayrami, it is especially jammed.

Another popular holiday is Children's Day, celebrated on April 23. Atatürk chose this date to honor children. His was the first country to observe this special holiday, which the United Nations has since recognized. Turkish citizens also celebrate National Sovereignty Day (Turkey's independence day) on this date. It marks the first meeting of Atatürk's Republican Party in Ankara. Children throughout the country, especially in large cities like Istanbul, take part in public gymnastic, dance, and choral performances.

Every November 10, people throughout Turkey observe two minutes of silence at 9:05 A.M. This event commemorates the time of Atatürk's death more than 60 years ago. In Istanbul's harbor, ferryboats sound their horns mournfully in honor of the late president and national hero.

Each year in June and July, residents of Istanbul gather for the Istanbul International Art and Cultural Festival. At this celebration, visitors can see all kinds of Turkish art, music, and dance.

Dancing dervishes
whirl at a festival in
Istanbul. Traditionally,
dervishes dance to
attain a mystical
union with God.

I was in a narrow room of marble, with a vaulted roof, and a fountain of warm and cold water; the atmosphere was in a steam, the choking sensation went off, and I felt a sort of pleasure presently in a soft boiling simmer, which, no doubt, potatoes feel when they are steaming.

—William Makepeace Thackeray, *Notes of a Journey from Cornhill to Grand Cairo* (1865)

The Turkish Bath

Since Roman times, Istanbul has maintained elaborate marble bathhouses for the public. Architects who constructed imperial mosques during Ottoman times also built luxurious public baths, called *hamams*, throughout the city. Like mosques, the hamams featured marble floors set beneath a large central dome surrounded by smaller domes. More than 100 bathhouses remain from the Ottoman era.

At the bathhouse, patrons enter a reception room for undressing in private, then a warm room for resting. The most elaborate part of the bath is a very hot room in a central domed hall with marble basins. Here attendants scoop flowing water from brass bowls and throw it on the bathers. In the center sits a large marble platform heated from below. Patrons lie on the platform to sweat and be massaged in one of the private cubicles. In Istanbul's most famous and beautiful bath, built in 1741 by Mahmud I, this central chamber is crowned with a dome supported on columns.

Neighborhood baths—like this one, built in the sixteenth century by the architect Sinan—are open daily all over Istanbul. Here bathers enjoy the invigorating effect of steam heat produced by boilers beneath the stone floor. Excess heat escapes through holes in the ceiling.

Baths are a family affair. Older boys go with their fathers, while girls and very young boys bathe with their mothers. In Turkish baths, men do not bathe naked. They wrap themselves in a waist cloth called a *pestemal*.

Women bathe nude in a separate section, or they use the bath on different days than the men do. For centuries, women who seldom left their homes frequented the baths. Besides bathing, they spent hours exchanging news, doing needlework, and sometimes inspecting potential daughters-in-law.

Besides the intense heat, another surprise to many Europeans and Americans is the rough cleansing they receive at the hands of bath attendants. Attendants clean patrons with bath gloves made of coarse cloth to remove layers of dead skin. The British novelist William Makepeace Thackeray said he felt he was being worked over violently with a horse brush.

Islam has always emphasized personal cleanliness, particularly before praying in a mosque. Until the 1920s, religious foundations owned the baths in Istanbul and kept them open to the public, free of charge. These days private owners run the baths, which attract an international clientele. One bath provides written instruction in more than five languages.

55

The Grand Bazaar

Ottoman Istanbul had many markets where goods from all over the world could be bought and sold. Specialized markets sold everything from spices to slaves. One market that still exists is the Grand Bazaar, the city's most famous general market.

A maze of stalls, restaurants, and warehouses, the Grand Bazaar is the largest indoor market in the world. Like a shopping mall, it offers a variety of goods for sale. Shoppers can find everything from blue jeans and sweat suits to Ottoman jewelry and antique carpets.

Entire streets of the bazaar are devoted to a single craft. Goldsmiths and silversmiths heap their wares in one lane, while rug and carpet merchants hawk their items in another. With 65 winding streets leading to cafés, fountains, shops, and a mosque, the Grand Bazaar is like a small village where one can easily get lost. The street names in this village include the Street of the Sword Makers and the Street of the Turban Makers. Sellers greet potential customers in many languages. Buying, selling, and bargaining are intense, yet transactions are social occasions that should not be hurried. Young boys are sent off to fetch glasses of tea, which are brought in anticipation of or after a purchase. More than half a million people shop in the Grand Bazaar every day. It has been a vital commercial hub for more than five hundred years. The city ensures that the bazaar is maintained and that merchants follow fair standards.

Like the city it serves, the Grand Bazaar has met and coped with disastrous earthquakes and fires. After the last major fire in 1954, the bazaar was quickly restored. But even with more up-to-date lighting, the Grand Bazaar remains a dark, mysterious place.

Exotic sights, sounds, and smells make the four thousand shops of the Grand Bazaar a tourist attraction (large image, facing page). Outside (left; insets, facing page) streets bustle with more stores and vendors peddling their goods.

I was plunged into a different world—the roar of traffic and the shouts of street urchins were instantly drowned in a sound barrage of Turkish music, water sellers' cries, the babble of business, and the din of people shouting....I wondered if I had not, for a moment, inadvertently stumbled upon Aladdin's Cave....
—Craig Mair,
twentieth-century historian

A Boat Ride from Europe to Asia

Steamers constantly weave up and down Istanbul's Bosporus Strait, making many stops and leaving ample time to get off and see sights. Not glamorous vessels, the inexpensive ferryboats are slow and crowded. It can take half a day for a steamer to loop the European and Asian sides of the Bosporus, which are only one-third of a mile to two miles apart. Apple tea and yogurt drinks are sold on the ferries. Vendors hawk socks or imitation

Rolex watches. Young boys offer shoe shines on portable brass stands.

As the ferryboat leaves the dock, passengers get a view of Beyoğlu, the newer section of Istanbul. Modern hotels, office buildings, and McDonald's restaurants dot the district. Beyoğlu also has older buildings, like the Galata Tower. On the water's edge is the opulent Dolmabache Palace. Still on the European side of the waterway stands Rumeli Hisari, a fortress built in 1452. Just

Open-air cafés—a haven for students and artists—surround the Ortakoy Mosque *(facing page)*. The city overlooks one of the world's busiest and most historic waterways, active with ferryboats *(below and right)* as well as large numbers of fishing and pleasure vessels.

beyond it rise two suspension bridges. The newer of these, named after Mehmed the Conqueror, is the third-longest suspension bridge in the world.

On the banks of the Bosporus are a garland of villages, some dating back to the time of Byzantium. In Ottoman times, Christian and Jewish minorities inhabited these once semirural villages. Many of these settlements have become suburbs of sprawling modern Istanbul. Magnificent mansions and summer homes lie on both shores. On the Asian side is the town of Anadolu Kavagi, famed for its fish restaurants. Here one can climb a castle to

view the Clashing Rocks, which mark the portal to the Black Sea. Much closer to Istanbul is Kadiköy, the largest of the Asian suburbs. One-third of Istanbul's citizens commute daily by boat or bridge from this suburb into the city.

As the ferryboat heads to its port, the sunset recreates the glow that earned the Golden Horn its name. It also backlights the city's mosque-dominated skyline. On the Galata Bridge, children and adults fish. Fishers sell seafood grilled right on their boats. Noisy and crowded, Istanbul seems like a fishing village once again.

Istanbul Timeline

	First Millennium B.C.	First Millennium A.D.	Second Millennium A.D.

1200–512 B.C.
Iron Age

C. 1200 B.C.	Mycenaean settlement on future site of Byzantium
657 B.C.	Founding of Byzantium by Byzas
512 B.C.	Byzantium falls to Persians

27 B.C.–A.D. 476
Roman Empire

A.D. 193–196	Lucius Septimus Severus sacks Byzantium and later rebuilds it.
A.D. 324	Constantine becomes head of Roman Empire.
A.D. 330	City of New Rome (the rebuilt Byzantium) officially inaugurated. City soon known as Constantinople
A.D. 410	Emperor Theodosius II builds new walls around Constantinople.
A.D. 476	Rome falls.

A.D. 476–1453
Byzantine Empire

A.D. 532	Nika Revolt. Justinian begins rebuilding city.
A.D. 537	Hagia Sophia rebuilt.
A.D. 717–787	Iconoclast Period (church icons destroyed)
A.D. 831–843	Final Iconoclast Period

A.D. 1054	Schism of Eastern Orthodox and Roman Catholic Churches
A.D. 1203	Fourth Crusade invades Constantinople.
A.D. 1261	Greek rule of Constantinople is restored.

Second Millennium A.D.

A.D. 1453–1922 Ottoman Empire	**A.D. 1453**	Ottoman Turks under Mehmed II conquer Constantinople. Byzantine emperor Constantine XI is killed in battle. Eastern Roman Empire ends.
	A.D. 1520–1566	Reign of Süleyman the Magnificent
	A.D. 1826	Abolition of Janissaries by Mahmud II
	A.D. 1914	Turkey sides with Germany in World War I.
	A.D. 1916	Turkish army led by Mustafa Kemal defeats Allied forces at Gallipoli.
	A.D. 1918	Allies defeat and occupy Turkey.
A.D. 1922– Modern Istanbul	**A.D. 1922**	Under Mustafa Kemal, Turkey wins War of Independence from Greece.
	A.D. 1923	Turkish Republic established. Capital transferred to Ankara. Sultanate abolished
	A.D. 1924	Turkish caliphate abolished
	A.D. 1928	Latin alphabet introduced to replace Arabic script
	A.D. 1930	Constantinople officially renamed Istanbul
	A.D. 1933	Kemal takes name Atatürk.
	A.D. 1934	Istanbul residents required to adopt surnames
	A.D. 1938	Death of Atatürk
	A.D. 1939–45	Turkey remains neutral but sides with Allies near end of World War II.
	A.D. 1946	Turkey joins the United Nations.
	A.D. 1952	Turkey joins NATO.
	A.D. 1982	New constitution adopted
	A.D. 1993–96	First woman prime minister of Turkey, Tansu Ciller, holds office.

Books about Turkey and Istanbul

Asi-Yonah, Avi. *Piece by Piece! Mosaics of the Ancient World*. Minneapolis: Runestone Press, 1993.

Baralt, Luis A. *Enchantment of the World: Turkey*. New York: Children's Press, 1997.

Feinstein, Steve. *Turkey in Pictures*. Minneapolis: Lerner Publications Company, 1998.

Freely, John. *Istanbul: The Imperial City*. London and New York: Penguin Books, 1998.

Godfrey, John. *1204, The Unholy Crusade*. New York: Oxford University Press, 1980.

Kelly, Laurence, ed. *Istanbul: A Traveler's Companion*. New York: Atheneum, 1987.

Knopf Guides: Istanbul. 4th ed. New York: Alfred A. Knopf, Inc. 1997.

Lye, Keith. *Take a Trip to Turkey*. London and New York: Franklin Watts, 1987.

MacDonald, Fiona. *A Sixteenth-Century Mosque*. New York: Peter Bedrick Books, 1994.

Settle, Mary Lee. *Turkish Reflections: A Biography of a Place*. New York: Prentice Hall, 1991.

Spencer, William. *The Land and People of Turkey*. New York: Lippincott, 1990.

Wheatcroft, Andrew. *The Ottomans*. New York: Viking, 1993.

Index

About the Author and Illustrator

Robert Bator is a retired college professor living in Chicago. He has visited Istanbul twice and has traveled to Greece, Japan, New Zealand, Fiji, and throughout Europe. In addition to travel, reading and photography are his favorite hobbies. Although he has taught children's literature and has written articles and books about Istanbul, this is his first book for children.

Chris Rothero of Oxford, England, studied art in Yorkshire and is a specialist in historical artwork. He has written books on medieval costume, and his artwork has appeared in the United Kingdom. He currently works with the Oxford Illustrators and Designers Group of Oxford, England.

Acknowledgments

For quoted material: p. 4, Laurence Kelly, ed. *Istanbul: A Traveller's Companion.* (New York: Atheneum, 1987); pp. 6, 28, Michael Maclagan. *The City of Constantinople.* (New York: Frederick A. Praeger, 1968); p. 9, John Freely. *Istanbul: The Imperial City.* (London: Penguin Books, 1998); p. 19, Robert Browning. *Justinian and Theodora.* (New York: Praeger Publishers, 1971); p. 21, Bernard McDonagh. *Blue Guide: Turkey.* (New York: W. W. Norton, 1995); p. 25, Elizabeth A. S. Dawes. *The Alexiad of the Princess Anna Comnena, Being the History of the Reign of Her Father, Alexius I, Emperor of the Romans, 1081–1118 A.D.* (London: K. Paul, Trench, Trubner and Co., Ltd., 1928); p. 31, Ernle Bradford. *The Great Betrayal: Constantinople, 1204.* (London: Hodder and Stoughton, 1967); pp. 35, 45, Clot, André. *Suleiman the Magnificent.* Translated by Matthew J. Reisz. (New York: New Amsterdam Books, 1992); pp. 37, 46, Andrew Wheatcroft. *The Ottomans.* (New York: Viking, 1991); p. 43, Philip Mansel. *Constantinople: City of the World's Desire, 1453–1924.* (New York: St. Martin's, 1996); p. 54, *Knopf Guides: Istanbul.* (New York: Alfred A. Knopf, Inc. 4th ed., 1997); p. 56, Mair, Craig. *A Time in Turkey.* (London: John Murray, 1973).

For photographs and fine art reproductions: Turkish Ministry of Tourism, pp. 4–5, 50, 51 (right), 58–59; Hermitage, St. Petersburg, Russia/Bridgeman Art Library, London/New York, pp. 10–11; San Vitale, Ravenna, Italy/Bridgeman Art Library, London/New York, pp. 14–15; Bridgeman Art Library, London/New York, p. 19, 39 (top), 41, 43; The Granger Collection, pp. 25, 30, 34–35; Robert Bator, pp. 22, 56, 57 (insets); Christie's Images, pp. 22 (inset), 23; Isabella Stewart Gardner Museum/Superstock, p. 25 (bottom); Art Resource, pp. 28–29; North Wind Pictures, pp. 31, 40–41; Victoria & Albert Museum, pp. 38, 46; Stapleton Collection, UK/ Bridgeman Art Library, London/New York, pp. 44–45; Mary Evans Picture Library, pp. 45, 46 (inset); © Chris Stowers/Panos Pictures, p. 51 (left); National Geographic Society, p. 54; © Bob Schatz/Liaison International, p. 57. Cover: Art Resource.